THE HALL OF STATUES

Wow! Look at these splendid statues! Each one has a matching pair ... except one thing has changed! Can you match the pairs, and then spot the differences?

First published 2019
by Walker Books Ltd
87 Vauxhall Walk
London SE11 5HJ

2 4 6 8 10 9 7 5 3 1

© 1987–2019 Martin Handford

The right of Martin Handford to be
identified as author/illustrator of
this work has been asserted by him
in accordance with the Copyright,
Designs and Patents Act 1988.

This book has been typeset
in Wallyfont and Optima.

Printed in China.

British Library Cataloguing in
Publication Data: a catalogue
record for this book is available
from the British Library.

ISBN 978-1-4063-8059-0

www.walker.co.uk

WALKER BOOKS
AND SUBSIDIARIES
LONDON • BOSTON • SYDNEY • AUCKLAND

WHERE'S WALLY?

DOUBLE TROUBLE

AT THE MUSEUM

MARTIN HANDFORD

Other than me and my friends, each
character appears in the queue twice.

But something has changed!

Can you spot all the differences?

WAY IN →

EVEN IN THE ENTRANCE HALL, THERE IS MAYHEM IN THE MUSEUM! CAN YOU SPOT ALL THE DIFFERENCES?

THE ENTRANCE HALL

Spot five differences among the security guards.

Spot five differences among the displays.

Spot five differences among the guests.

15 DIFFERENCES

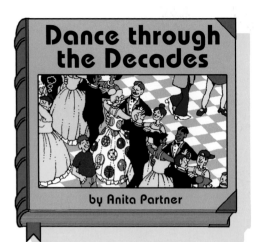

Dance through the Decades
by Anita Partner

Musical Methods
by Dewey Sing

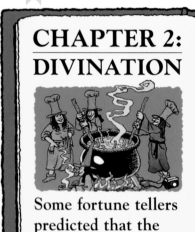

CHAPTER 2:
DIVINATION

Some fortune tellers predicted that the future was coming.

A Guide to Brush Work
by Horace Shu

Ivanna Scare
HAUNTED HAPPENINGS

Sir Cumference
KNIGHTS TO REMEMBER

Musical Methods
by Dewey Sing

A History of
Horticulture
by Dan DeLion

TREASURES TO TREASURE
BY EMMA RULD

Many dinosaurs roamed the earth.

One herbivorous dinosaur was the Triceratops.

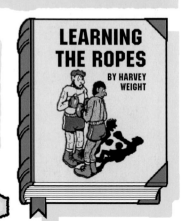

LEARNING THE ROPES
BY HARVEY WEIGHT

THE READING ROOM

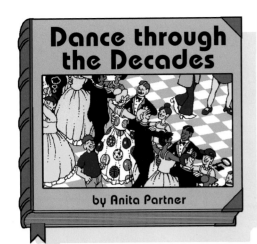

Dance through the Decades
by Anita Partner

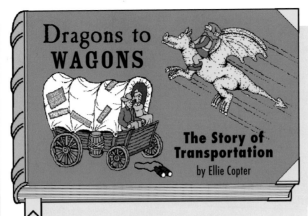

Dragons to WAGONS
The Story of Transportation
by Ellie Copter

A Guide to Brush Work by Horace Shu

A SHORT HISTORY OF TIME
T. K. Tock

TREASURES TO TREASURE
BY EMMA RULD

Many dinosaurs roamed the earth.

One herbivorous dinosaur was the Tricerabottoms.

Ivanna Scare
HAUNTED HAPPENINGS

LEARNING THE ROPES
BY HARVEY WEIGHT

Sir Cumference
KNIGHTS TO FORGET

A LONG HISTORY OF TIME
T. K. Tock

A History of Horticulture
by Dan DeLion

CHAPTER 2: DIVINATION

Some fortune tellers predicted that the future was coming.

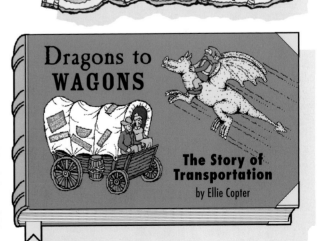

Dragons to WAGONS
The Story of Transportation
by Ellie Copter

18 DIFFERENCES

THE EGYPTIAN ROOM

Spot eight differences between each pair of tablets.

16 DIFFERENCES

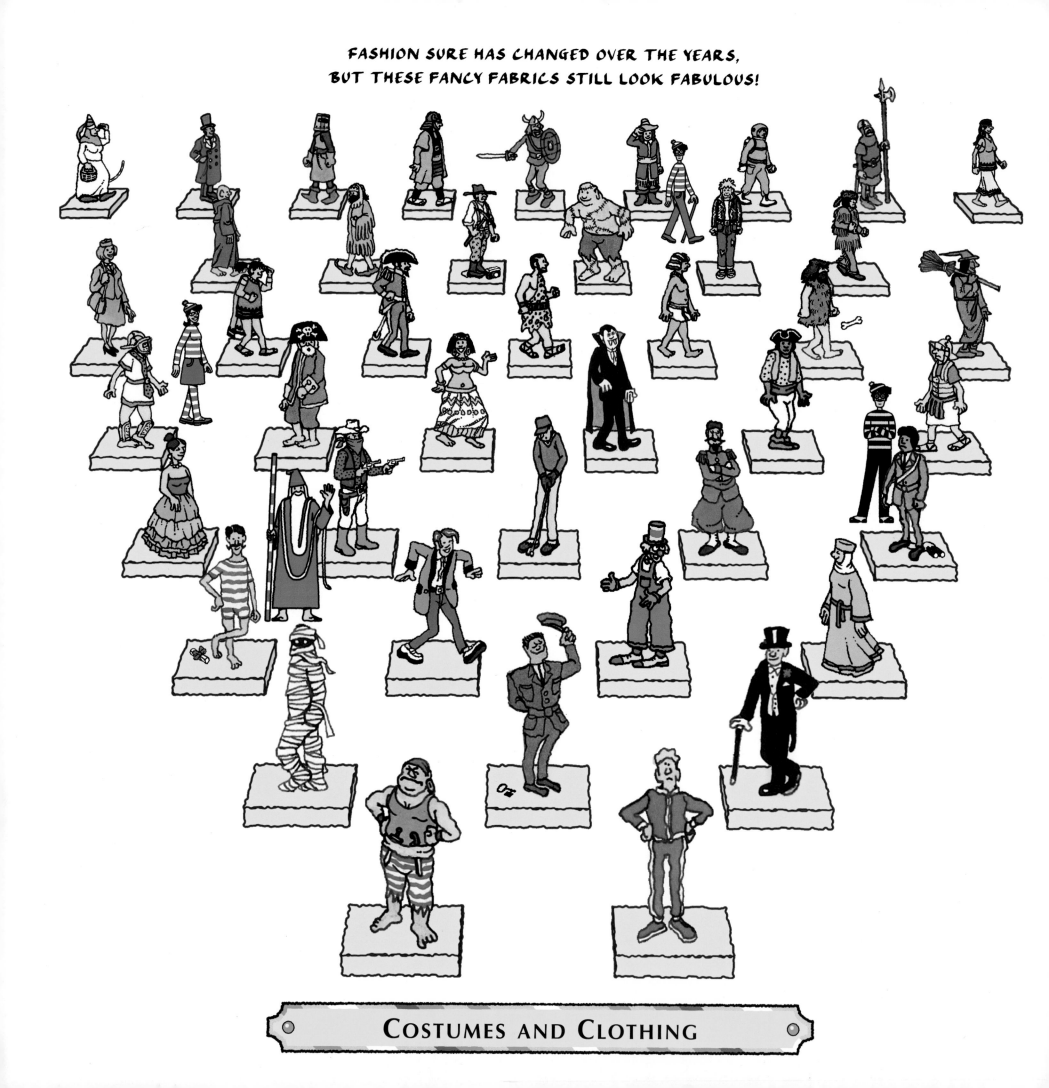

FASHION SURE HAS CHANGED OVER THE YEARS,
BUT THESE FANCY FABRICS STILL LOOK FABULOUS!

COSTUMES AND CLOTHING

Spot the difference between each costume.

42 DIFFERENCES

THE MARITIME COLLECTION

Spot five differences between each seascape.

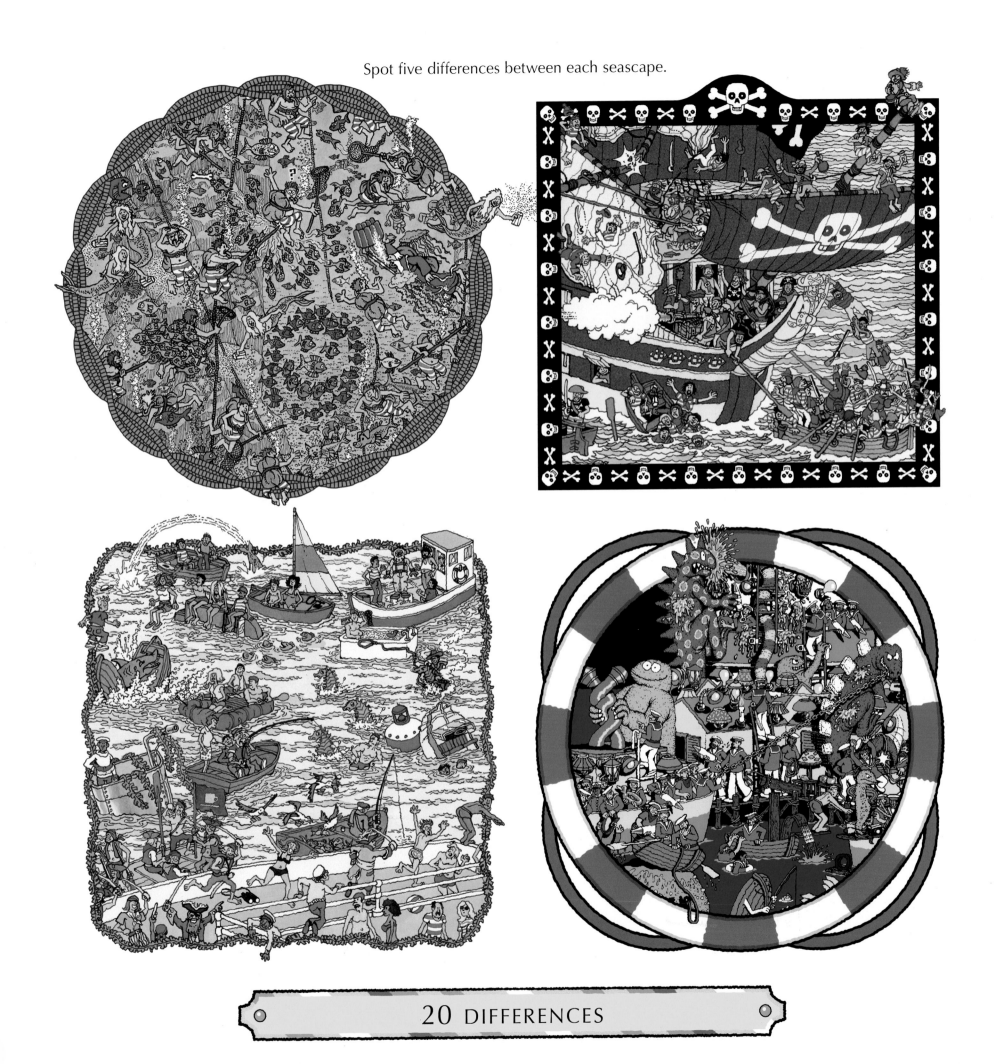

20 DIFFERENCES

SOMETHING'S A BIT OFF-KEY HERE. YOU'LL NEED TO CONDUCT A PROPER SEARCH TO FIND ALL THE DIFFERENCES. STAY SHARP!

Spot six differences among the pink army.

Spot six differences among the blue army.

MUSIC AND MELODY

Spot six differences among the drummers.

Spot two more differences ... somewhere!

20 DIFFERENCES

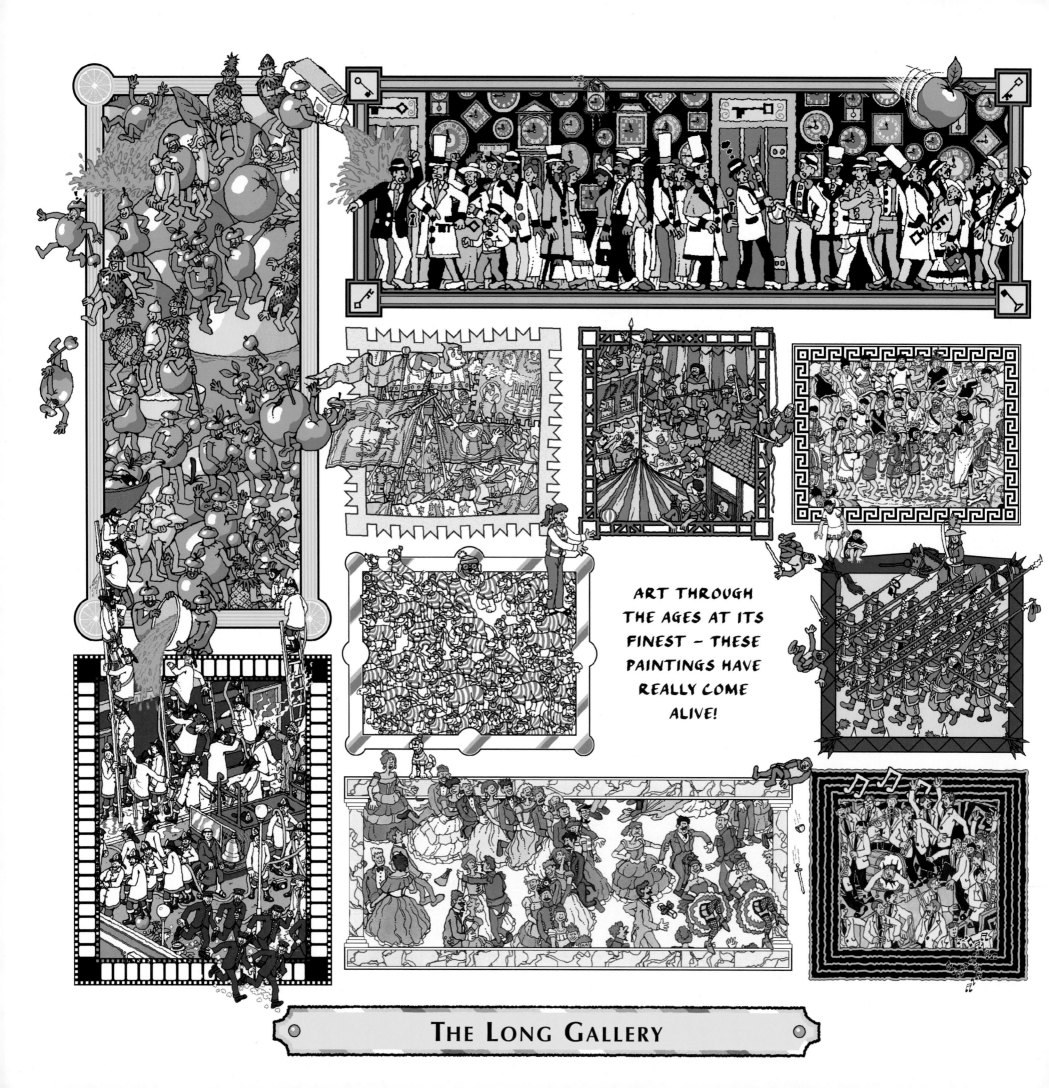

ART THROUGH THE AGES AT ITS FINEST – THESE PAINTINGS HAVE REALLY COME ALIVE!

THE LONG GALLERY

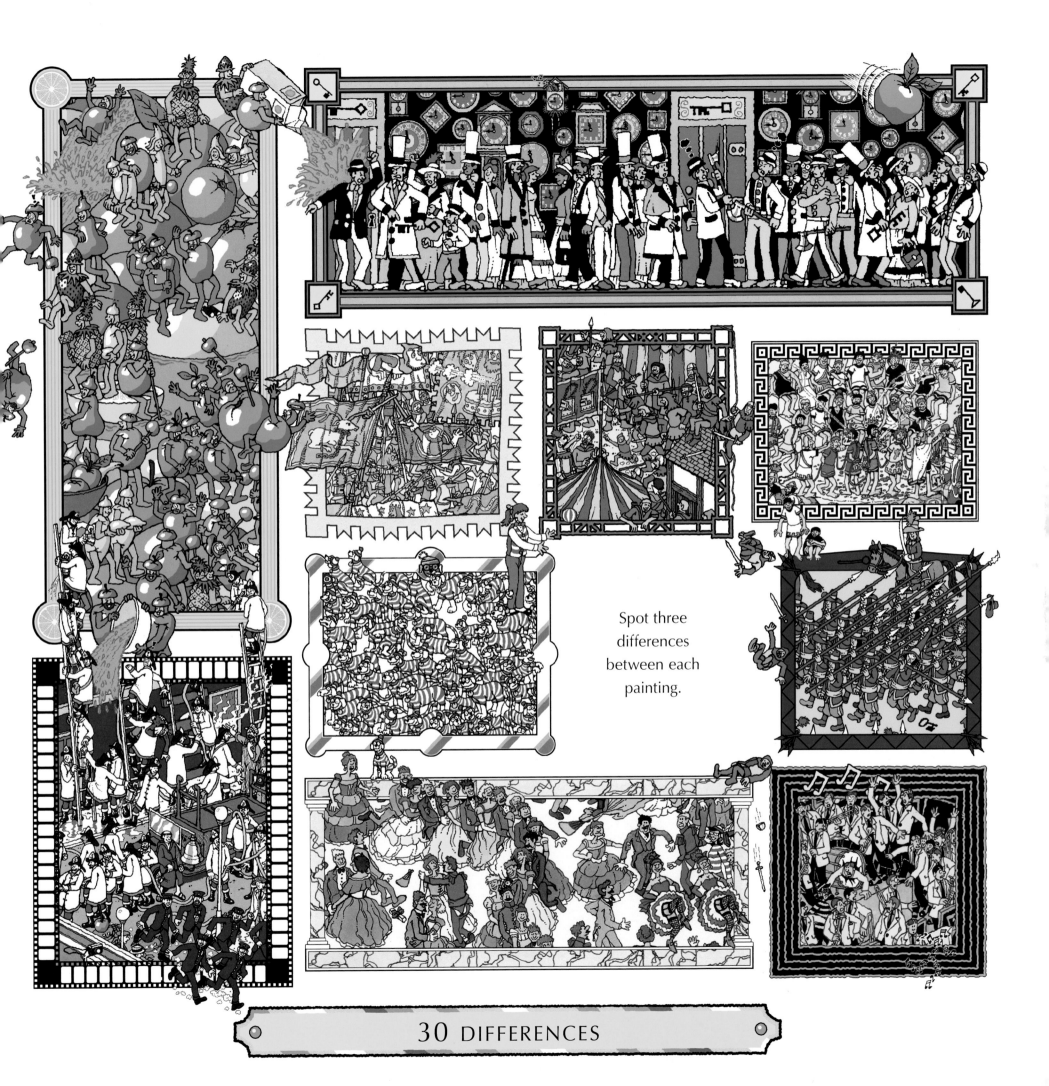

Spot three differences between each painting.

30 DIFFERENCES

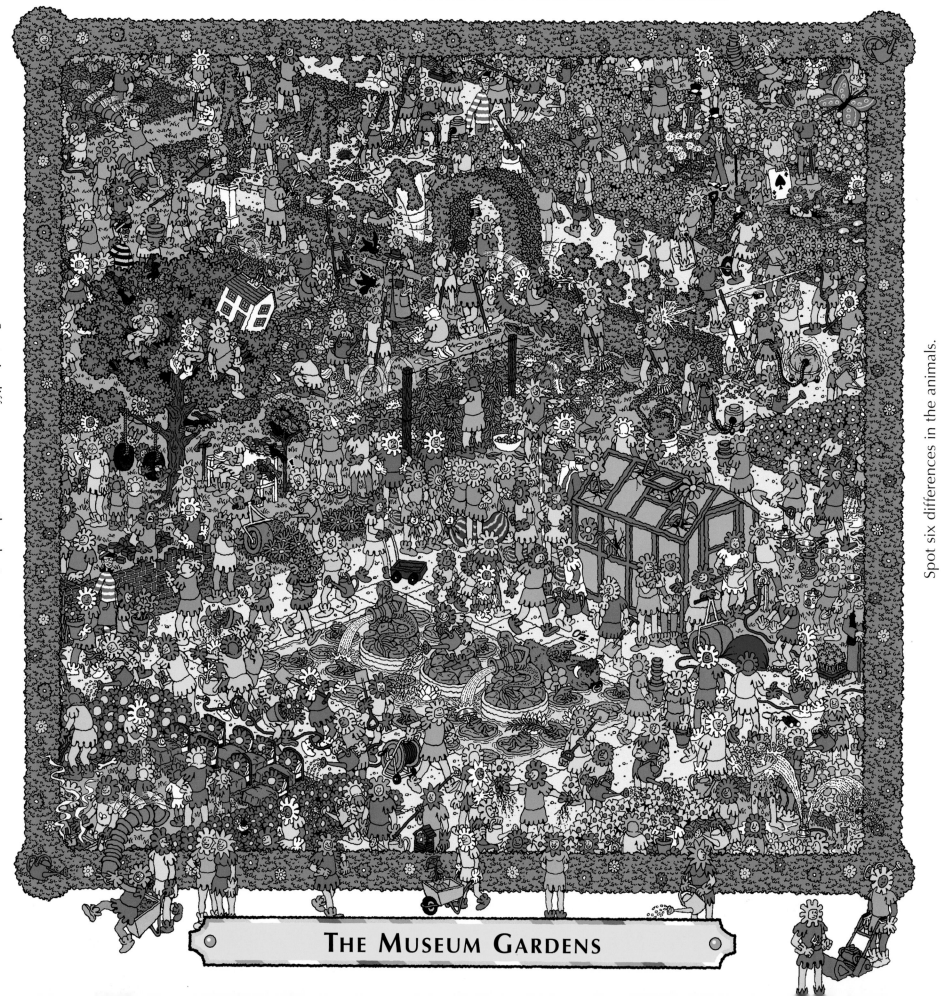

Spot six differences among the plants.

Spot six differences in the animals.

THE MUSEUM GARDENS

Spot six differences in the topiaries.

Spot six differences among the flower people.

Spot six more differences ... somewhere!

30 DIFFERENCES

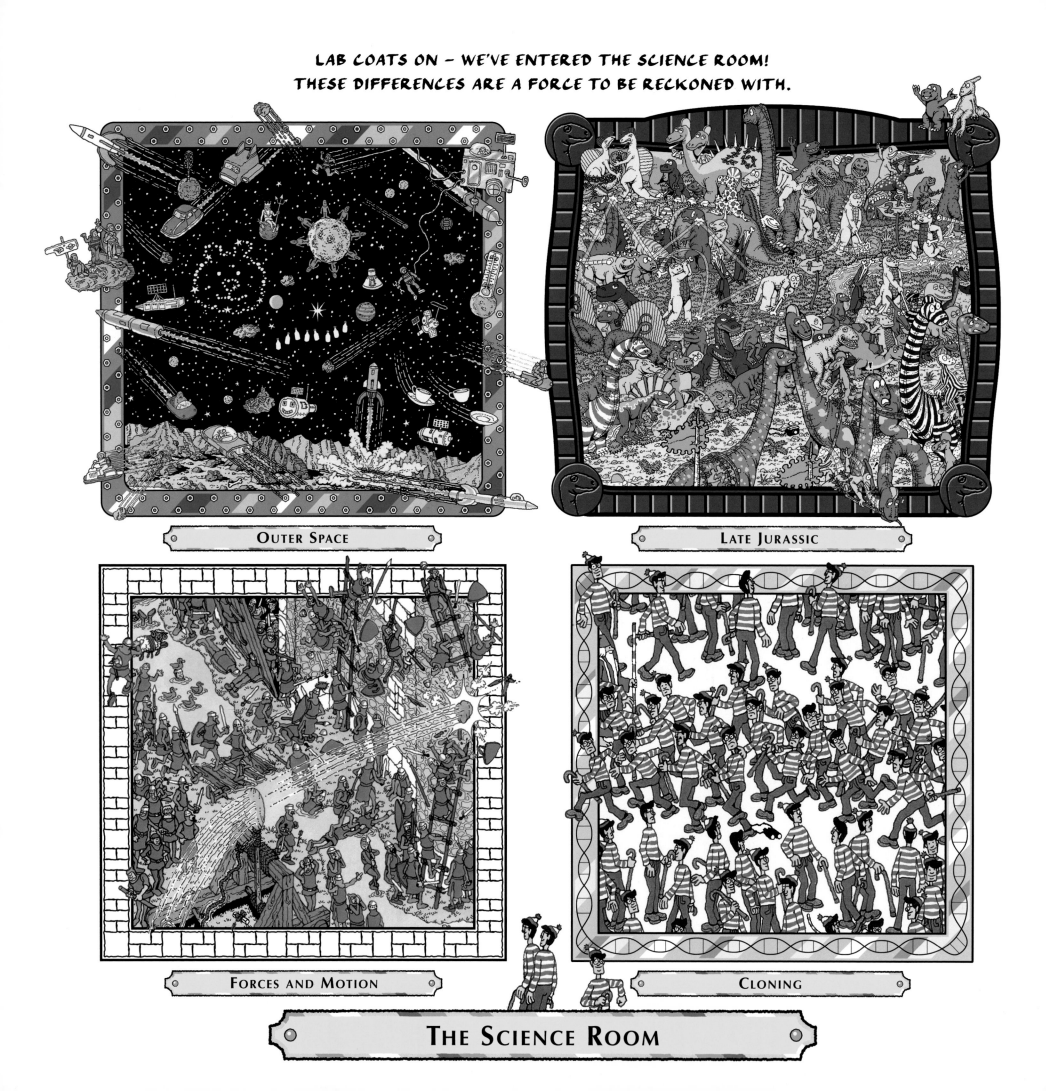

LAB COATS ON – WE'VE ENTERED THE SCIENCE ROOM!
THESE DIFFERENCES ARE A FORCE TO BE RECKONED WITH.

OUTER SPACE

LATE JURASSIC

FORCES AND MOTION

CLONING

THE SCIENCE ROOM

Spot five differences between each exhibition.

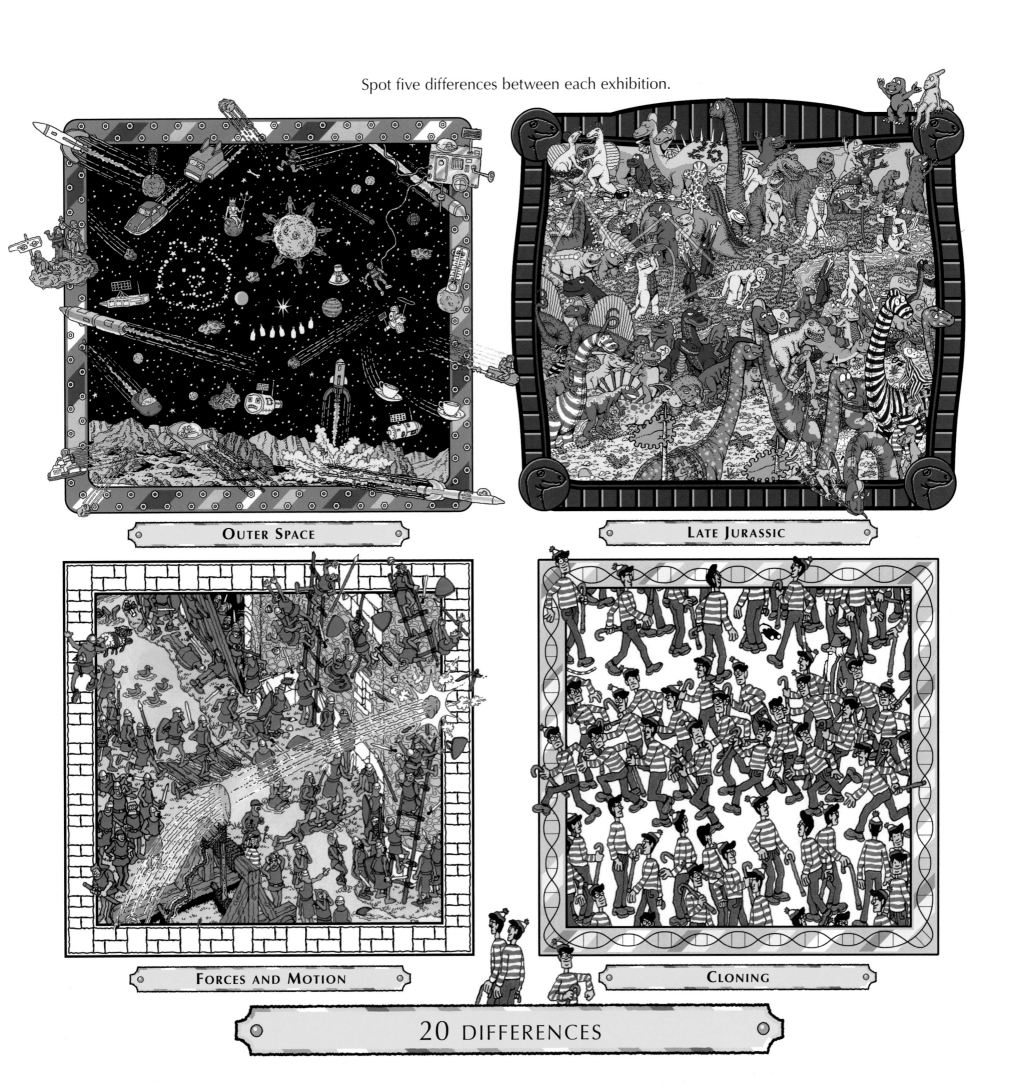

OUTER SPACE

LATE JURASSIC

FORCES AND MOTION

CLONING

20 DIFFERENCES

MY SKETCHES

SOME OF THE FLOWERS WEREN'T BLOOMING ...

FORTUNATELY, THE GARDENERS GOT TO THE ROOT OF THE PROBLEM.

MAGNIFICENT AND MYSTERIOUS MONUMENTS!

FUN AT THE CASTLE ...

WITH A GREAT KNIGHT LIFE!

WHAT A FANTASTIC FLAG!

FEARLESS AND FEROCIOUS VIKINGS, BARGE!

THIS EXHIBIT WAS DINO-MITE!

LOTS OF POTS!

MAGNIFICENT AND MYSTERIOUS MONUMENTS!

HERE ARE MY OWN SKETCHES FROM AROUND THE MUSEUM!

Spot two differences between each sketch.

26 DIFFERENCES

WHAT A WONDERFUL DAY AT THE MUSEUM! AND THERE'S STILL
TIME FOR A QUICK TRIP TO THE GIFT SHOP!

Find the ten hidden yellow scrolls, and where they've moved to in the picture on the opposite page.

Spot ten differences in the souvenirs.

THE GIFT SHOP

Spot ten differences in the shoppers.

Spot ten new characters on this side who have arrived from somewhere else in the museum, then find which pages they came from!

40 DIFFERENCES

WHERE'S WALLY?

DOUBLE TROUBLE

AT THE MUSEUM

MARTIN HANDFORD

CHECKLISTS

Now that you've spotted all the differences, here are several more things to look for!

ONE LAST THING

Each picture has one matching pair ... except two things have changed! Can you spot the difference?

ONE FINAL, FINAL THING

Turn to the front cover of the book and look at the paintings above the museum balcony. Each painting has a pair – can you spot a total of 22 differences between them?

THE ENTRANCE HALL

- [ ] A collapsing pillar
- [ ] A robbery in progress
- [ ] A dog on a lead
- [ ] Charioteers
- [ ] A drummer
- [ ] A toppling row of pots
- [ ] A poking painting
- [ ] Two shields
- [ ] Someone doing a handstand
- [ ] Someone in love with a person in a portrait

THE READING ROOM

- [ ] A ball gown
- [ ] A bag piper
- [ ] A horse-drawn carriage
- [ ] Shadow boxers
- [ ] A crocodile face
- [ ] Shrinking portions
- [ ] A waving dinosaur
- [ ] A red watering can
- [ ] A yellow watering can
- [ ] A bow tie

THE EGYPTIAN ROOM

- [ ] A thirsty sphinx
- [ ] Two horses
- [ ] A very loud horn
- [ ] Two sarcophagi
- [ ] A picture firing an arrow
- [ ] Dates falling from a tree
- [ ] Two angry snakes
- [ ] An upside down stretcher
- [ ] Six workers pushing a block of stone

COSTUMES AND CLOTHING

- [ ] One statue wearing green shoes
- [ ] Five statues wearing gloves
- [ ] Three statues with earrings
- [ ] Costumes with stripes
- [ ] Costumes with spots
- [ ] Costumes with buttons
- [ ] Costumes with belts
- [ ] Three skull-and-crossbones
- [ ] A blue bandana
- [ ] A red shield

THE MARITIME COLLECTION

- [ ] Five golden swords
- [ ] A catfish
- [ ] A dogfish
- [ ] Four seagulls
- [ ] A cowboy riding a seahorse
- [ ] An inflatable duck ring
- [ ] A bathtub
- [ ] A leaky diving suit
- [ ] An anchor
- [ ] A candle